Corinne Bailey rae

Wise Publications
part of The Music Sales Group

London / New York / Paris / Sydney / Copenhagen / Berlin / Madrid / Tokyo

Published by
Wise Publications
8/9 Frith Street, London, W1D 3JB, England.

Exclusive distributors:
Music Sales Limited
Distribution Centre, Newmarket Road,
Bury St Edmunds, Suffolk, IP33 3YB, England.

Music Sales Pty Limited
120 Rothschild Avenue, Rosebery, NSW 2018, Australia.

Order No. AM985391
ISBN 1-84609-510-7

Music arranged by Derek Jones.
Music processed by Paul Ewers Music Design.
Edited by Chris Harvey.
Printed in the EU.

www.musicsales.com

Your Guarantee of Quality:
As publishers, we strive to produce every book
to the highest commercial standards.

The music has been freshly engraved and the book has
been carefully designed to minimise awkward page turns and
to make playing from it a real pleasure. Particular care has
been given to specifying acid-free, neutral-sized paper made
from pulps which have not been elemental chlorine bleached.

This pulp is from farmed sustainable forests and
was produced with special regard for the environment.

Throughout, the printing and binding have been planned
to ensure a sturdy, attractive publication which should give
years of enjoyment.

If your copy fails to meet our high standards, please inform us
and we will gladly replace it.

'Like A Star'

Words & Music by Corinne Bailey Rae

enchantment

Words & Music by Corinne Bailey Rae & Rod Bowkett

game where you're giv - ing chase._ Guess it could be called an ac - qui - red taste._

I know he knows, he calls, I go,___ I know.___

This could be an en - chant - ment. Why don't you tell___

___ me? I'm___ for - giv - en. He calls,___ don't__

15

Put Your Records On

Words & Music by Corinne Bailey Rae, John Beck & Steven Chrisanthou

'Till it happens to you

Words & Music by Corinne Bailey Rae, Paul Herman & Pamela Sheyne

1. I know_____ what I said_____ was heat of_____ the mo - ment._____
2. Went to_____ the old flat,_____ guess I was try-in' to turn the clock back. But how comes that no - thing feels the same now when I'm

There's a lit - tle truth in be -

22

24

'Trouble Sleeping'

Words & Music by Corinne Bailey Rae, John Beck & Steven Chrisanthou

'Call Me When You Get This'

Words & Music by Corinne Bailey Rae & Steve Bush

1. How does it feel_____ being_____ in these___
2. I've got all this po-et-ry_____ now,__
3. I just want-ed to know what_____ it was__

35

Ooh,____ so____ much more each day, ba - by, if you're

still a - wake,____ call me when you get this._____

Fade out

'Choux pastry heart'

Words & Music by Corinne Bailey Rae & Teitur Lassen

1. I was just wait-ing for your phone-call

when they came a-long to say that a rose done chased

you clear a-way.

'Breathless'

Words & Music by Corinne Bailey Rae & Marc Nelkin

1. Seems like ev-'ry-one else has a love just for them._
2. I can un-der-stand that you don't want to cross the line.

I don't mind, we have such a good time, my best friend._____
And you know I can't pro-mise you things will turn out fine._____

Amaj7 F#m7 B7

But some-times, well, I wish we could be more than friends._____
But I have to be ho-nest, I want you to be mine._____

Bbmaj7 N.C. F#m7 B7 Bm7

Tell me do you know?_____ Tell me do you know?_____

Bbmaj7 A %Dm9 Cmaj9

_____ I get__ so breath-less__ when you call__ my__

E7sus4 A Dm9 Cmaj9

name. I've of-ten won-dered:__ do you feel__ the__

42

Words & Music by Corinne Bailey Rae, Paul Herman & Thomas Danvers

Me and Can-dice wak-ing up____ to a heat - wave.
Used to spend our Sum-mer hav - ing par-ties on the drive.

1° only

Mo-ther's in the gar - den____ in - vit-ing ev - 'ry - one.____ Ooh,____

____ we cut off our own jeans____ and go out - side.____

Em⁹   A⁷

Neigh-bour's al - ways smil-ing with a ba - by on her knee.
Plas-tic cups____ for rum and punch, eat-ing chick-en that's hot and sweet. All the

47

51

Butterfly

Words & Music by Corinne Bailey Rae & Rod Bowkett

Seasons Change

Words & Music by Corinne Bailey Rae & Steve Brown

2 3 4 5 6 7 8 9
5/06(58920)